• Contents •

• About the Life Skills Series •

This series aims to provide the busy classroom teacher with practical ideas and strategies for developing and enhancing a set of valuable life skills in individual students.

There are numerous resources and articles about teaching values, dealing with grief, addressing bullying and the like, however, most of these articles and programs outline strategies for dealing with the problem at the whole-school level. While this is indeed a very appropriate way to deal with such matters, it has become obvious that there is a lack of ready-to-use materials for the actual classroom teacher. The Life Skills Series aims to fill the gap between the frameworks set out by national bodies and the delivery of practical and meaningful lessons in the classroom.

The Life Skills Series comprises four books:

Self Esteem and Values
- Enhancing self esteem of individuals
- Developing an awareness of feelings
- Promoting realistic goal-setting
- Enriching values in the classroom and community

Grief, Illness and Other Issues
- Coping with grief and loss
- Dealing with a disability or serious illness

Bullying and Conflict
- Coping with bullying at school
- Exploring conflict resolution through a problem solving approach

Family Relationships
- Discussing family roles
- Dealing with anger and other emotions
- Coping with separation, divorce and conflict

Each of the books in this series should be used as required. The series is not structured to be a complete program of work. Instead, it is designed as a valuable and practical resource for teachers that find themselves with students who are going through difficult life events.

Most of the activities are stand-alone – it is up to the teacher to decide what sheets will be relevant to the class. Some sheets will only be relevant to a select number of students, e.g. a bereaved student or a student who belongs to a blended family.

The themes in these four books overlap and so, when dealing with a particular issue, e.g. conflict resolution, activities from other books in this series might also be relevant to the situation that may exist in your classroom.

As well as student worksheets, all books contain extensive background notes for teachers, parents and students. Several sections contain annotated guides to relevant websites and literature resources available both online and in hard copy. Also included are extension ideas and teaching ideas for the classroom. The activities are linked to relevant student outcomes (see Pages 5-9).

Internet References

Websites that are included in these four books can be accessed easily by visiting:

▶ www.aber-publishing.co.uk

Bookmark this page for ease of use. ▶ info@aber-publishing.co.uk

Changing Lives

Grief, Illness & Other Issues

- Coping with grief and loss
- Dealing with a disability or serious illness

By Jar

Life Skills Series

Grief, Illness and Other Issues

(BLM)

© 2010 Jane Bourke

ISBN: 978-1-84285-181-4

Author: Jane Bourke
Typesetting & Design: Vikatan Publishing Solutions Pvt. Ltd.
Artwork: Terry Allen

Disclaimer

The material given in this book is given in good faith. Readers are advised that websites change and that readers should take professional advice before entering into any arrangements with outside providers mentioned here or elsewhere. The publishers GLMP Ltd, nor any/all of their agents nor the author can be held responsible for outcomes resulting from contact with any organizations mentioned herein. Teachers using this book with students are requested to make this clear to students and their parents.

Published by:
AberEducation
P.O. Box 225
Abergele
Conwy County LL18 9AY
UK

Aber Education

• Curriculum Links •

Subjects Areas and Strands

National Curriculum: non statutory guidelines for PSHE at key stage 3
Knowledge, skills and understanding

Developing confidence and responsibility and making the most of their abilities

1) Pupils should be taught:
   a. to reflect on and assess their strengths in relation to personality, work and leisure
   b. to respect the differences between people as they develop their own sense of identity
   c. to recognise how others see them, and be able to give and receive constructive feedback and praise
   d. to recognise the stages of emotions associated with loss and change caused by death, divorce, separation and new family members, and how to deal positively with the strength of their feelings in different situations
   e. to relate job opportunities to their personal qualifications and skills, and understand how the choices they will make at key stage 4 should be based not only on knowledge of their personal strengths and aptitudes, but also on the changing world of work
   f. to plan realistic targets for key stage 4, seeking out information and asking for help with career plans
   g. what influences how we spend or save money and how to become competent at managing personal money.

Developing a healthy, safer lifestyle

2) Pupils should be taught:
   a. to recognise the physical and emotional changes that take place at puberty and how to manage these changes in a positive way
   b. how to keep healthy and what influences health including the media
   c. basic facts and laws, including school rules, about alcohol and tobacco, illegal substances and the risks of misusing prescribed drugs
   d. in a context of the importance of relationships, about human reproduction, contraception, sexually transmitted infections, HIV and high-risk behaviours including early sexual activity
   e. to recognise and mange risk and make safer choices about healthy lifestyles, different environments and travel
   f. to recognise when pressure from others threatens their personal safety and well-being, and to develop effective ways of resisting pressures, including knowing when and where to get help
   g. basic emergency aid procedures and where to get help and support.

Developing good relationships and respecting the differences between people

3) Pupils should be taught:
   a. about the effects of all types of stereotyping, prejudice, bullying, racism and discrimination and how to challenge them assertively
   b. how to empathise with people different from themselves
   c. about the nature of friendship and how to make and keep friends
   d. to recognise some of the cultural norms in society, including the range of lifestyles and relationships

e. the changing nature of, and pressure on, relationships with friends and family, and when and how to seek help
f. about the role and importance of marriage in family relationships
g. about the role and feelings of parents and carers and the value of family life
h. to recognise that goodwill is essential to positive and constructive relationships
i. to negotiate within relationships, recognising that actions have consequences, and when and how to make compromises
j. to resist pressure to do wrong, to recognise when others need help and how to support them
k. to communicate confidently with their peers and adults

Breadth of study

4) During the key stage, pupils should be taught the Knowledge, skills and understanding through opportunities to:
   a. take responsibility [for example, for carrying out tasks and meeting deadlines such as taking assembly, running the school newspaper]
   b. feel positive about themselves [for example, by taking part in a public performance]
   c. participate [for example, in developing and putting into practice school policies about anti-bullying; in an action research project designed to reduce crime and improve personal safety in their neighbourhood]
   d. make real choices and decisions [for example, about options for their future, based on their own research and career portfolios]
   e. meet and work with people [for example, people who can give them reliable information about health and safety issues, such as school nurses, community drug awareness workers]
   f. develop relationships [for example, by working together in a range of groups and social settings with their peers and others; by being responsible for a mini-enterprise scheme as part of a small group]
   g. consider social and moral dilemmas [for example, how the choices they make as consumers affect other people's economies and environments]
   h. find information and advice [for example, about the risks of early sexual activity, drug misuse, self-defence for keeping safe]
   i. prepare for change [for example, by anticipating problems caused by changing family relationships and friendships, and by preparing for new styles of learning at key stage 4].

Notes

During key stage 3 pupils learn about themselves as growing and changing individuals and as members of their communities with more maturity, independence and power. They become more self-aware, and are capable of more sophisticated moral reasoning. They take more responsibility for themselves and become more aware of the views, needs and rights of people of all ages. They build on the experience, confidence and competence they developed in key stage 2, learning new skills to help them make decisions and play an active part in their personal and social life. They learn how to plan and manage choices for their courses and career. They continue to develop and maintain a healthy lifestyle, coping well with their changing bodies and feelings. They also learn to cope with changing relationships and understand how these can affect their health and well-being. They make the most of new opportunities to take part in the life of the school and its communities.

Hey Thompson

Developing Self Esteem and Resilience in Secondary School Students

A Manual for Mentors

Information Points

- Authoritative- written by an experienced teacher and expert
- A growing issue in schools and colleges
- Targeted mailing to schools
- Photocopiable content making it great value for money
- Trials show the book is very popular with teachers

Life Skills- An Aber Education Series

This title has been written for any individual who is undertaking a mentoring role with a secondary school student. This book provides strategies and organisational guidelines for mentoring. There is significant evidence of widespread concern about the current economic pressures that are permeating society, particularly in the current economic climate. Such pressures are felt by young people who often feel they cannot cope, that is why this book is so important.

The book contains:

- An explanation of The Thompson Self-Esteem Model
- A discussion on the role of the mentor
- The student performance profiler
- Self esteem and learning performance
- Self esteem and the ability to socialise and communicate self to others
- The ideal image, developing a sense of direction
- Strategies and Activities to assist Students to Develop resilience

Market

All teachers

- 11-16-Level teachers and FE College young trainees
- Adult education centres
- Teachers, tutors and lecturers
- School libraries, reference and public libraries
- University and college central libraries.
- Designed for KS3 and 4 teachers and post 16/FE student mentors.

Related Titles

Self Esteem and Values	*978-1-84285-182-1*
Grief, Illness and other issues	*978-1-84285-181-4*
Bullying and Conflict	*978-1-84285-179-1*

Author	Lou Thompson
Price	£24.99
Format	Paperback, A4 photocopiable 170 + pages
Isbn	978-1-84285-178-4
Territory	UK, Europe, South Africa,

'I get to see a lot of books; just occasionally a gem appears. One where the approach is grounded in work from real classrooms, by real teachers. This book is one of those gems, I strongly recommend it to all teachers.'

Dr Graham Lawler

aka the Radio broadcaster Mr Educator and BBC Bitesize Maths author

Aber publishing

Books to Improve Your Life

Self Esteem
Understanding a complex phenomenon,
A Manual for Mentors

Selling Points

- Authoritative- written by an experienced professional
- A growing issue in schools and colleges
- Targeted mailing to schools
- A vital component in staff training for whole school improvement
- Trials show the book is very popular with teachers

Life Skills- An Aber Education Series

This title is part of a new life skills series from Aber Publishing but this title is slightly different in that it is written for mentors rather than mentees. To maximise their role as 'significant others', self-esteem mentors need to have a sound and pragmatic understanding of the self-esteem phenomenon. In the literature, debate, confusion and conjecture abounds. The explanation and working model presented highlights key considerations and principles and is intended to provide self-esteem mentors with a pragmatic framework within which to work at enhancing the self esteem of children and young people.

The book contains:

- Why we should be concerned about youth self-esteem
- Identifying and assisting children with special self-esteem needs
- The importance of mentors self esteem
- The importance of quality leisure and time management
- Role play activities which help students reflect and adjust their self image.

Market

- All teachers
- Student teachers and FE College lecturers
- Education centres
- School staff libraries,
- reference and public libraries
- educational psychologists
- youth leaders and youth workers
- apprentice trainers

Author	Lou Thompson
Price	£14.99
Format	Paperback, A4 photocopiable
Isbn	978-1-84285-177-7
Territory	UK, Europe, South Africa,

Related Titles

Self Esteem and Values	978-1-84285-182-1
Family Relationships	978-1-84285-180-7
Grief, Illness and other issues	978-1-84285-181-4
Hey Thompson	978-1-84285-178-4
Bullying and Conflict	978-1-84285-179-1

About the Author

Lou Thompson is a well-respected expert in the development of positive self-esteem in young people. He is a keen sportsman and is a family man

Aber publishing
Books to Improve Your Life

This book has been designed to provide ideas and strategies for dealing with difficult situations that students must sometimes endure. There may be situations that arise within your classroom or school environment that need special consideration.

Examples include:

❑ The death of a class member or school student (road accident, illness, terrorism and so on);

❑ A student or relative may be diagnosed with a potentially life-threatening illness such as leukaemia;

❑ A student may have trouble dealing with the issue of adoption;

❑ A student or a student's relative or family member may become disabled after an accident;

❑ A student/s may be victims of a traumatic event (e.g. a terrorist attack);

❑ A student's relative or family member may die (e.g. baby death from SIDS).

The approach of this book involves providing a realistic "scenario" for each of the issues as a basis for promoting discussion and learning opportunities specific to the issue. Some of the scenarios may be particularly relevant to individual class members, while other students may be exposed to such issues for the first time.

The issues raised in the following stories and activities are designed to promote whole class discussion. Certain activities are designed to be used as a follow-up to the "scenario" while other sheets have been included so that the students can discuss and reflect upon these issues based on their own experiences. The sheets are ideal for homework activities for students to complete in their own time. Encourage students to discuss the sheets with their parents/guardians. Students can later reflect on their ideas and thoughts as a whole class or in small groups.

The sheets can also be used as whole class Health activity or as needed. For example, following a death in the family, you may wish to give a grieving student sheets to complete on their own or with family members.

The activities in this book can also be used with students who have no direct experience with grief and loss. It can help them to understand what a grieving person is feeling, as well as preparing them for situations where they themselves may have to cope with a tragedy within their family or circle of friends.

Strategies for the Classroom

Encourage openness and honesty in the classroom. Whole class and small group discussions are helpful for students who feel they are alone in their suffering. For example, students who are coping with a newly-diagnosed illness will greatly benefit from hearing others' stories. If possible organise for a cancer survivor to be a guest speaker.

The same can be said about students whose parents are separating or divorcing. Students who are adopted can display a range of reactions and need to discuss their feelings with their classmates and teacher.

It is intended that these sheets be dealt with at the teacher's discretion and in conjunction with counselling from qualified school counsellors. The sheets do not provide any special remedies for dealing with grief and loss. They are designed to facilitate discussion and to promote a friendly classroom climate for exchanging thoughts and ideas. The main aim of the activities is to allow students to see that their reactions to certain events are normal and that grieving is a necessary process.

When a class member experiences loss and grief, the class and even the whole school community can be affected. Children will be affected in different ways and their behaviour will provide clues as to how they are dealing with their emotions and thoughts. A range of behaviours may be displayed including withdrawal, aggressiveness, anger, fear, stress and panic. Many students may experience guilt stemming from the fact that they believe they caused the loss. In other circumstances, students may feel guilty about being alive and healthy.

Most grieving students will be preoccupied with other thoughts and will find it difficult to stay on task or concentrate, thus evoking a decline in schoolwork. As the teacher, it is best to remain patient and understanding of the processes that a grieving student is working through.

Set up a place in the classroom or adjoining area where a bereaved student can retreat to if necessary. Ideally this will be a quiet place and other students should be advised of this area to respect the grieving process.

Encourage students to write stories and poems and to create pictures to express their grief. Even though only one student may be grieving, the class functions as a group and sharing grief may benefit the entire class. Empathising with students affected by grief and loss can provide learning opportunities for all students, particularly for students who have never been exposed to loss and death. Create a class book of poems and encourage caring and open discussion so that the grieving student does not feel isolated and alone.

Avoid treating the grieving student/s differently by rewarding them unnecessarily. Students will want to be seen as a part of a group and will not want to be treated differently or put into a situation where other students will see the treatment as unfair.

Find out if there are other students at the school who have experienced a similar loss and encourage the development of a peer support group.

Gather some appropriate resources from the library or from the list on Page 15. These could be used as a whole class resource or for individual students.

Communicate clearly with the family of a grieving student and keep them informed of students' class progress.

In situations where student/s at the school have died, acknowledge this as a whole school unit and create a memory of the student by planting a special tree or something similar.

Students may grieve:

- ❑ when a parent, grandparent or sibling dies;
- ❑ when a family breaks up;
- ❑ when they become physically handicapped;
- ❑ after moving house or to a new town/country;
- ❑ when separated from a parent for a long period of time;
- ❑ after a burglary, particularly if they lost something precious to them;
- ❑ after a natural disaster such as fire, flood or cyclone – students may grieve for their loss of memories.

Please note:

Some worksheets in this book are designed to be used only with students who have experienced a loss, been diagnosed with an illness or suffered a disability. (See Page 31 **My Story** for an example.)

Discuss:

- ❑ Taking care of health. Grieving can take its toll on the body. Ensure students get enough rest and participate in exercise. Encourage healthy eating to keep stress levels down.

- ❑ If students are facing major decisions, such as deciding on school subjects or sporting endeavours, ask them to postpone their choices if possible, until they are able to think more clearly.

- ❑ Explain to the student that he/she must be patient as he/she goes through the grieving process and that there is no definitive time frame for when grief stops.

- ❑ Ask grieving students to try to be patient with other students, particularly those students who have no understanding of grief and loss.

- ❑ Encourage students to return to the normal daily routines. This will help them to stop focusing on the grief that could lead students into a depression.

- ❑ If a family member has died, there will be lots of arrangements that need to be made and possibly younger siblings to take care of. It is important that the grieving student makes time for him/herself and tries to remain calm.

- ❑ Eventually the student will let go of the grief and move on. Explain to the student that this is OK. This new phase will allow them to get back on track with their normal life and to remember the person they lost, rather than merely focusing on the death.

For Teachers: Looking After Yourself

The issues raised in the Life Skills series, particularly in this book, can seriously impact on the teacher who has to face such issues with a class. Situations described in the front of this book, such as the death of a student, can take their toll on the classroom teacher in several forms. It is important that teachers remember to take some time out to process their own emotions and thoughts on the issues that can sometimes arise in their classroom.

Teachers in such positions may develop symptoms of stress. Some common reactions can include:

- ❑ Feelings of anger and frustration directed at students, parents and other staff members;

- ❑ Feelings of inadequacy regarding ability to cope with difficult situations;

- ❑ Feelings of guilt when a positive outcome is not achieved;

- ❑ Feelings of helplessness or depression that may cause insomnia, loss of appetite and loss of concentration.

After critical incidents, opportunities for debriefing and consulting with support staff should be given, to help prevent or minimise stress-related symptoms.

It is important that teachers accept the things that they cannot change rather than trying to take responsibility for something they have no control over.

Useful websites:

- ▸ **www.nswtf.org.au/OH&S/stress.html**
  - Work Related Stress
- ▸ **aca.ninemsn.com.au/stories/1648.asp**
  - Managing Stress
- ▸ **cms.curriculum.edu.au/mindmatters/ resources/pdf/booklets/loss_intro.pdf**
  - Loss and Grief
- ▸ **www.aare.edu.au/02pap/how02342.htm**
  - Resilient Teachers: Avoiding Stress and Burnout
- ▸ **www.jweducation.com/childstress.ppt**
  - Child Stress (Powerpoint Presentation)

Families, Friends and Feelings

▸ **www.cyh.com/cyh/kids/index.html**
CYH Kids Only. Contains interesting and detailed sections on being part of a family providing a range of family unit situations, as well as sections on health, nutrition, body issues, school, friends, emotions and adolescence.

▸ **kotn.ntu.ac.uk/allabout/friends/index.cfm**
Kids on the Net: A Celebration of Friendship.

Students can read what other children have written about friendship and are able to post their own ideas. Includes poems, stories and essays.

▸ **www.henry.k12.ga.us/pges/kid-pages/friendship/default.html**
This site is aimed at children and explores the friendships that students make, problems that friendships endure and ways that conflict can be resolved. There is also an online survey for students to complete. The information should be used with the teacher as a starting point for group discussion.

Grief and Loss

▸ **www.griefworksbc.com/SiblingDeath.asp**
Death of a sister or brother.

▸ **www.asiblingssite.com/**
This site is dedicated to children who may have a sibling with a chronic illness.

▸ **www.death-dying.com/children/**
Children and Grief. This site is dedicated to helping children and teens through the difficult process of grieving the loss of a loved one, friend, pet or relative.

▸ **www.bbc.co.uk/health/kids/** - An informative web reference for kids created by the BBC. Contains information on a range of issues dealing with both the body and mind. The Body section examines aspects such as caring for the body with information on smoking, drugs, alcohol, nutrition and exercise. The Mind section explores the areas of friends, home, school, changes and loss.

▸ **www.connectforkids.org/usr_doc/CopingWithGrief.htm** - Contains resources for helping kids cope with trauma.

▸ **www.aidskids.org/** - An American website set up for children with AIDS.

Coping With Disabilities

▸ *Copingwithdisability.com*
this website is all about *coping* effectively with a *disability* or health problem. *www.copingwithdisability.com/* - Cached - Similar

▸ *Coping* **with illness pain and** *disability.* **Help comfort and support.**
Surviving *disability,* pain and sickness.Best links for the disabled,physically challenged,long-term sick,their carers and families. *www.soon.org.uk/problems/disability.htm* - Cached - Similar

▸ *Coping with disabilities - Life Coaching*
Don't let disabilities slow you down. - *Coping with disabilities - Life Coaching* is a personally written site at BellaOnline. *www.bellaonline.com/articles/art30884.asp* - Cached - Similar

▸ **The ABC's of** *coping with disability*
The ABC's of *coping with disability.* ... B, Build support systems -- professional/other people with similar disabilities. ... *www.americanheart.org/presenter.jhtml?identifier=2871* - Cached - Similar

▸ *Coping With Disability*
"*Coping With Disability*" is one of many topics covered by the handicap tips at LifeTips. *handicap.lifetips.com/cat/56385/coping-with-disability/index.html* - Cached

▸ [PDF]
1247 3 Coping with disability
File Format: PDF/Adobe Acrobat - Quick View minor work done in your home by the Handyperson and have no other needs. Tel: 020 8314 6309. 4. *Coping with disability* – equipment and adaptations ... *www.lewisham.gov.uk/NR/.../0/12473Copingwithdisability.pdf* - Similar.

Conflict

1. **Teen Suicide Prevention**
Evidence-based research articles focusing on teen **suicide** prevention *www.TPRonline.org*

2. **Suicide Help?**
Know someone who might be **suicidal?**
Call HOPELineUK 0800 068 41 41
www.papyrus-uk.org

3. **You Can Avoid Suicide**
Find hope and life instead of despair and death
www.suicide-is-not-painless.info

- **www.allkidsgrieve.org/**
  A valuable resource for teachers, parents, counsellors and caring adults.

- **www.relate.org.uk**
  An excellent background resource for teachers and parents with sections on coping with divorce, step families, coping with change and so on. Much of the information deals with adult relationships, however, there are some interesting sections that explain how to guide children through difficult aspects of relationships.

- **www.familymanagement.com/**
  A useful family resource with articles on a number of areas such as dealing with grief, relatives, disasters and so on.

- **http://goodgrief.org/** They say
  The Shiva Foundation was formed to open the dialogue around issues of grief and loss in such a way that honors loss in the cycle of life. The Hindu god Shiva dances the cosmic dance of creation and destruction teaching us that each act of destruction calls for an act of creation. We take that into our grief to teach us that we heal our loss through acts of creation.

- **www.opendoorcounselling.org.uk**
  Open Doors. Counselling and Education Services.

- **www.skylight.org.nz**
  Skylight Trust. Suitable for teachers, this New Zealand website is from the Skylight organisation. Skylight supports children and young adults facing grief, loss and change in their lives. Contains international links as well as NZ contacts.

- **www.personalwellbeingcentre.org**
  They say
  We are a social enterprise that aims to promote the well-being and growth of individuals, organisations and communities through education, training and one-to-one work

- **www.rainbows.org/rainbows.html**
  An international, non-profit organisation that fosters emotional healing among children grieving a loss from a life-altering crisis.

- **www.hospicenet.org/html/talking.html**
  Includes useful information about how to talk to children about death and loss.

- **www.dougy.org/**
  The Dougy Centre for Grieving Children and Teens

- **www.opendoors.com.au/AdolescentGrieving/AdolescentGrieving.htm**
  Grief in Adolescence

- **www.grief.org.au/internetl.html**
  Centre for Grief Education: Links

- **www.sandswa.org.au/grief/grief1.html**
  Children's Grief - Coping with SIDS.

- **users.erols.com/lgold/info.htm**
  Deals with "complicated" grief, where children have failed to express or resolve significant life issues.

- **www.adec.org/** association for death education and counselling, US site.

INTRODUCTION

Literature for Students

- The Dougy Center, (1983) _35 Ways to Help a Grieving Child_, The Dougy Center for Grieving Children, 3909 SE 52nd Ave, Portland OR 97206, USA. ISBN: 189053403X

- Harris, Christine (2001) _Jamil's Shadow_, Puffin, Australia. ISBN: 141312106

- Metzenthen, David (2000) _The Colour of Sunshine_, Penguin, Australia. ISBN: 0-7320-2602-4

- Broome, Errol (2001) _Cry of the Karri_, Allen & Unwin, Australia. ISBN: 18650840

These titles below all contain collections of stories from children and teens that openly discuss their feelings and direct experiences with the issues:

- Krementz, Jill (1988) _How it Feels When a Parent Dies,_ Knopf Random House Inc., New York, USA. ISBN: 0394758544

- Krementz, Jill (1988) _How it Feels to be Adopted_, Knopf Random House Inc., New York, USA. ISBN: 0394758536

- Krementz, Jill (1988) _How it Feels When Parents Divorce_, Knopf Random House Inc., New York, USA. ISBN: 0394758552

Teacher Resources

- Irving, Tricia, _When Tough Stuff Happens_, Available from the Skylight Trust. New Zealand. **www.skylight.org.nz**

- _Talking to Children About Death_, Available from The Outstretched Hands Publications. Sydney: Telephone (02) 4567 2156.

- Mason, Hillary (2003) _Cancertalk_ (Primary and Secondary Packs), Macmillan Cancer Relief. **www.macmillan.org.uk/ classaction**

Online Specialist Book Sellers

- **www.compassionbooks.com/** - Compassion Books, USA.

Stories Online

- **www.layouth.com/4_03_3_1.htm** - Story: _My Brother's Death Changed My Family Forever_

INTRODUCTION

Chloe's Story

Chloe had just turned ten years old when she started to feel unwell. She couldn't believe how tired she was and she felt someone had drained all the energy out of her body. She also noticed that she had a strange number of bruises appearing and she couldn't quite remember how she got them. At first, she thought it was just a bug but she noticed she was starting to feel worse each day instead of starting to feel better. Each night when Chloe went to bed, she'd imagine that she would wake up the next day and feel on top of the world. But when she woke up the next day she felt worse than ever.

Chloe's mother made a doctor's appointment for her and she underwent several tests including a blood test. A few days later, Chloe went back for a follow-up visit and this time her dad went too. The doctor asked to speak to Chloe's parents first. When they came out of the doctor's office, Chloe noticed her mum had been crying. She gave Chloe a hug and said "We love you and you are going to be OK". Chloe suddenly began to feel scared.

Chloe and her parents went into the doctor's office and the doctor told Chloe that she had a rare childhood disease called leukaemia. Chloe learned that this disease was going to require her to undergo months of treatment. She found out that leukaemia is a form of cancer that occurs when human cells – that make up the tissues and organs in the human body – divide and multiply abnormally. Chloe also learnt that part of the treatment would involve having chemotherapy, which meant she would be injected with powerful drugs over a long period of time. The drugs were designed to target cells that were dividing rapidly, however, sometimes these drugs affect normal healthy cells, which is why chemotherapy often comes with a lot of harsh side effects, such as feeling nauseous and having your hair fall out.

When Chloe first found out about her illness, she immediately thought she was going to die. She had heard of other people who had been diagnosed with cancer who were no longer around. There had been a boy in Year 3 at her school, Thomas, who had died at the end of Term 2. Chloe hadn't really known Thomas but she remembered being very sad when she heard about his death. The school held a special service and some children in Thomas' class had planted a tree for him in the front garden of the school grounds. Chloe suddenly wondered if there would be a tree planted in her honour, before quickly snapping out her trance. "I will beat this disease!" she said to herself, "No trees for me!"

The doctor told Chloe that there was a very good chance of her making a full recovery, however, he said they would have to see how her body responded to the treatment. The treatment for Chloe's leukaemia required her to stay in hospital for some time and attend an out patient clinic. The special ward at the hospital – known as the Oncology and Haematology Unit – was full of children who had similar cancers and Chloe made many new friends. Her school friends came to visit her but they didn't quite understand what Chloe was going through and some of her friends would get sad when they saw all of the other cancer patients, especially the ones who had lost their hair and had swollen faces from the drugs. Some of the other patients were around Chloe's age and the hospital used to have special activities for them to do. They also had plenty of visitors such as sporting stars and visiting celebrities. Their ward was lucky enough to have a fun centre that had been donated by the Starlight Children's Foundation. They even had teachers on the ward, to help the kids keep up with their schoolwork!

However, Chloe's time in hospital wasn't all fun and games. Each day she had to have intensive chemotherapy and lots of other medical procedures. Sometimes the drugs went straight into her veins via a drip. Chloe felt very sick for a lot of the time and there were times where she thought she was never going to get better.

While Chloe was in hospital she kept a diary. She started the diary the day she was first diagnosed and made time to write each day. She had always been good at writing and felt that sometimes it was easier to express her feelings through writing rather than by trying to talk to people. There were some days when Chloe felt so sick that she couldn't possibly write a journal entry, so on these days she asked other cancer patients to write something for her for that day. Each month Chloe would read what she had written. She started to notice her ideas about her disease changing over time. She looked back at some of the earlier entries where she had worried about dying and the pain she was going to go through. She thought to herself that she now felt more positive and concentrated on getting better.

Chloe was told that if her treatment was successful she would go into "remission". Basically, this meant that the abnormal white blood cells would not be detected in her blood or bone marrow, and that normal bone marrow would start to develop again. Being in remission didn't mean that all of Chloe's troubles were over though, as there would still be other harmful cells floating around her body. The doctor explained that Chloe would need to keep taking "maintenance" drugs to destroy these cells. The good news was that if Chloe made it into remission, she wouldn't have to be in hospital to take this medicine. She would, however, have to return to the hospital for regular check ups and special blood tests for a number of years.

Chloe was really hoping her hair would grow back by Christmas. In her diary, Chloe also made a list of everything she wanted to do once she was in remission and was well enough to leave the hospital. She decided she would keep writing in her diary as it gave her something to look forward to each day. She asked each of her "cancer" friends to write a poem about their feelings and she spent a lot of time decorating her diary, both with photos and drawings. She even asked the doctors to write something!

When Chloe left the hospital seven months later, she was approached by a cancer fundraising charity that had heard about her diary through the staff at the hospital. The charity asked Chloe if she was interested in getting her book published. At first Chloe didn't know what to make of this request. For a start, she had written the diary for herself –it had all her thoughts and feelings inside. She wasn't entirely sure if she wanted anyone to read the whole diary. She thought about it for a while and she reread her diary several times over that week. Even though Chloe had explained in great detail how horrible the chemotherapy was, she had also included all of the happy times that had occurred, and of course she had written all about the new friends she had made in hospital. Chloe decided that she wanted her diary to be published.

The charity organisation covered all of the publishing costs for Chloe's book and sold *Chloe's Diary* to hospitals, libraries and schools, not just in Chloe's city, but all over *Chloe's Diary* became very popular with kids' cancer support groups and for other kids who had just found out that they had leukaemia. When Chloe was well enough to go to other schools to talk about her experience with the disease. She had her picture in the paper and was even asked to go on television to talk about her illness. Chloe always remembered to mention all of the people she had met who were going through a similar experience. She did not want people to think she was the only person who had ever been sick with leukaemia. Instead, she wanted to draw attention to the illness, so that other children understood what the disease was about and that it could be beaten.

Chloe still had a lot of treatment ahead of her and continued to keep a diary. She made a point of going back to the cancer ward that she had spent so much time in, both to visit some old friends and also to talk to new patients.

The money raised from *Chloe's Diary* was donated to the hospital so that doctors could carry out research for new treatments for leukaemia. Some of the money was given to the cancer ward.

Further Reading:

▸ **www.macmillan.org.uk/whybother/**
- Excellent site from Macmillan Cancer Relief

▸ **www.kidscancernetwork.org/**
- Kids Cancer Network

▸ **www.starlight.org.au/grownups/whatwedosfc.cfm**
- Read about Starlight Fun Centres

▸ **www.cancerbacup.org.uk/Aboutcancer**
- All About Cancer

Websites:

▸ **www.asiblingssite.com/**
- This site is dedicated to children who may have a sibling with a chronic illness.

Activity 1	Reflection: Chloe's Story

❶ What sort of cancer did Chloe have?

_____

_____

❷ Write down everything you learnt about this disease from reading the story.

_____

_____

_____

_____

_____

_____

_____

❸ What did Chloe's treatment involve?

_____

_____

_____

_____

_____

_____

❹ Describe Chloe's attitude towards her illness

_____

_____

_____

_____

_____

❺ How did Chloe cope with her illness?

_____

_____

_____

_____

_____

_____

_____

_____

❻ If you were in Chloe's shoes, what would your reactions have been when told about the disease? Discuss.

_____

_____

_____

_____

_____

_____

_____

_____

Did You Know?

- 4 in 10 people will develop cancer at some time stage of their life.
- Cancer can occur in any part of the body.
- Most people affected by cancer are usually over the age of 60, and it is rare to develop cancer at a young age.
- Sometimes people find it difficult to talk to people who have cancer.
- Not everybody dies when they are diagnosed with cancer. There is often a large chance of recovery.

Activity 2	Family Reactions

☞ *When a person is diagnosed with a serious illness, a lot of people who are close to that person can be affected. Family and friends often find it hard to cope when someone close to them is sick and they can feel very sad and helpless.*

Imagine if Chloe was a member of your family. Write down what you think some reactions might be for the people below. Include ideas about how you think people might cope when someone close to them has a serious illness.

Joanne (Chloe's older sister):

Hannah (Chloe's best friend):

Chloe's parents:

Chloe's classmates:

? How do you think Chloe's family coped with her illness?

_____

_____

Activity 3 — Lost for Words

☞ *Many people don't know what to say to people who have a very serious illness. Sometimes people can feel guilty about being healthy. Sometimes people can feel very sad as they think the sick person might not get better. Sometimes they can feel angry that this person is suffering.*

❶ Think about times where you have had to talk to someone who has a serious illness. What did you say to them? Explain how you felt about talking to them. (e.g. nervous, afraid, angry, shy, sad.)

What do I say? ...

_____

_____

_____

_____

_____

_____

_____

❸ How could you help someone who was diagnosed with a serious illness. List some things you could do.

_____

_____

_____

_____

_____

_____

_____

_____

❷ What do you think might happen to someone who has had cancer or any other serious illness, once he/she is well enough to go back to the school? Include some of the changes that might have occurred while he/she was in hospital.

_____

_____

_____

_____

_____

_____

❹ How would you like to be treated if you found that you had a serious illness? What would you expect your friends and family members to do or say?

_____

_____

_____

_____

_____

_____

Activity 4	Changed Lives

☞ *Sometimes people don't recover from cancer. You or someone else at your school may know someone who has died from cancer. This person may be someone's mother, sister, father or brother. You may have even lost a family member or best friend to cancer.*

❶ **Think about how you can talk to someone who has experienced the loss of a loved one from a serious illness. What might you say?**

_____

_____

_____

_____

_____

❷ **There are many ways you could show a friend that you care about him/her at this sad time. Some of these things include writing stories, writing poems, drawing pictures and making up songs to remember this special person. How do you think these things might help?**

_____

_____

_____

_____

_____

❸ **What would you choose to do to help a friend who had lost someone who was close to them?**

_____

_____

_____

_____

_____

❹ **Do you think you would like to share your feelings with other people or would you rather spend time alone, thinking to yourself?**

_____

_____

_____

_____

_____

_____

_____

? A Public Display of Grief

When Princess Diana died in August, 1997, almost the whole country was grieving for her loss. It was a very sad time and even though most of the people had never even met her personally, they were very upset and displayed their emotions in public. Why do you think this was the case?

_____

_____

_____

Aber Education

Activity 5	A Range of Reactions

☞ *Look back at Chloe's story and think about the different emotions and attitudes that Chloe experienced from the time she was diagnosed until the time she was able to leave the hospital.*

Write down examples of positive and negative reactions in the table below.

Negative Reactions	Positive Reactions
e.g. thinking of the pain	e.g. thinking about getting better
−	+

In this second table, write down how you think YOU would react if you were in Chloe's situation. If you have experienced an illness like Chloe's, try to remember how you felt at the time.

Negative Reactions	Positive Reactions
−	+

In this last table, think of a situation involving someone you know who has had a serious illness. List some of the reactions of this person, their family, friends and classmates.

Negative Reactions	Positive Reactions
−	+

Sporting Moments

Jamie had been kicking a football around for as long as he could remember. One of his earliest memories was handballing with his dad, Robert, down at the park on Aberdeen St. His dad was a champion league player and had only just retired from playing professional football. He now had all the time in the world to go for a kick with Jamie, in fact, he now had time to take over the coaching position of Jamie's under 14s team.

Aside from being the eldest of four children, Jamie was also the only boy in the family himself. He was very proud of his dad's achievements on the field and hoped to one day play league football himself. His dream was to play for his dad's team and to wear the number 24, just like his dad. Robert had helped Jamie every step of the way, taking him to football clinics, camps and of course to the big games to watch his old team.

One chilly August morning, Robert and Jamie set off for the match they had been waiting for. It was Jamie's big game, and the winning under 14s team would go straight into the grand final. Jamie was quietly confident that his team were going to win but he tried not to show it. They had played their competitors twice already this year, winning both times, but by very narrow margins. The last time the two sides met, Jamie had kicked the winning goal after the siren had sounded for the final quarter. The crowd had cheered and car horns beeped. It had been one of Robert's proudest moments.

Jamie could barely sit still on the drive to the playing field. Robert told him to calm down but Jamie kept going on and on about how this game meant everything. The team had worked so hard to get to this point and that if they didn't go out there and win today, it was going to be a waste of all of the hard work they'd put in. Robert gave Jamie the same advice he'd heard a dozen times before. "Jamie, I just want you to go out there and play your best. You've played a big role in getting the team to this stage of the competition. If you win, that's fantastic but if you lose it's not going to be the end of the world. You're only young, you've got plenty of grand finals to look forward to."

As soon as the car pulled up at the club, Jamie leapt out of the car door and headed for the change rooms to see the boys. Everyone was fired up, some were nervous, some were playing it cool, and some boys were acting like it was just any other game. The main thing on the boys' minds was the weather and the fact that they were going to be swimming in a pool of mud before the game was over!

The rain had begun to pour down and the boys had to shout over the noise of the rain bucketing down on the tin roof of the club.

Jamie suddenly realised that in all his excitement, he'd left his socks and football boots in the boot of his dad's car and there were only minutes to spare before the team was supposed to run onto the field. He bolted out of the change rooms, into the pouring rain and ran straight into the path of a four-wheel drive.

***

Jamie woke up in a dimly lit hospital room. His mind immediately drifted to his last memory — being at the playing field, talking to Johnno in the change rooms and getting ready for the game. "I must have been knocked unconscious during the game," he thought to himself. Jamie couldn't move. His neck was in a brace. There was no one in the room, but there were nurses and doctors passing by about outside.

It was at that precise moment that Jamie realised he couldn't feel anything in his legs. He tried to wiggle his toes but he had no idea where to even start. He tried concentrating on flexing his calf muscles but he may as well have been submerged in a pile of ice-cold jelly as he could feel absolutely nothing. He did notice though that he could feel and move his arms and he quickly pressed a button on the remote sensor that had been placed in his hand.

The doctor explained to Jamie that he had been involved in an accident. She went on to tell him he had suffered a cervical spine injury and that he had what was known as "intercostal nerve paralysis". This meant that he would not be able to use his legs as a result of the injuries he sustained in the accident. Jamie was stunned. He didn't know what to say. There were a million questions he wanted to ask, but he didn't think he wanted to know the answers. He had no idea what "intercostal nerve paralysis" meant but it didn't sound at all good.

Eventually, Jamie summoned the courage to ask the doctor whether he would ever walk again. The doctor paused before explaining to Jamie that he had already been in hospital for three days in a coma. She told him the damage to his spinal cord was severe and that tests were still being carried out. Finally, she said that while the damage looked to be permanent, there was some chance that in the future he might be able to walk after extensive rehabilitation. The doctor held Jamie's hand and looked him in the eyes as she told him there were no guarantees.

Jamie didn't know where to start. He thought it must all be a bad dream. A nightmare.

He tried to feel his feet again, his knees, his calves, ANYTHING. He drifted off to sleep, his mind a blur of questions and thoughts. When Jamie woke up his family were gathered around the bed. Jamie's father Robert had red eyes and his mother looked as though she had aged five years.

"You gave us such a fright, we're so glad you woke up." His mother barely got the words out before bursting into tears.

"Don't cry Mum, I am going to be OK," said Jamie trying to put on a brave face. "And Dad, did we win the game?"

***

Jamie stayed in hospital for six months. His spine needed to be stabilised and he was given steroids to make sure his neurological system could function properly. Jamie had learnt all about his neurological system during the six months. He asked the nurses and doctors all sorts of questions. By the end of his hospital stay, Jamie knew all the scientific terms for the affected parts of his body. When his mates came to visit him and asked how he was, no one quite knew what Jamie was talking about!

The day came when Jamie was moved from intensive care to a special rehabilitation ward. He was lucky not to have sustained brain damage as a result of the injury to his spinal cord. Once his spine had stabilised Jamie was allowed to start a rehabilitation program.

During the six months that Jamie was in hospital, his parents organised renovations to make their house wheelchair accessible. Robert even had a lift installed so that Jamie could easily get to his bedroom upstairs.

***

After two years, Jamie was still not able to use his legs. No feeling had returned and months of rehabilitation had showed that there was little hope of him regaining any control over his lower limbs. Jamie was determined to walk again one day, but right now he thought he would try and focus on other achievements he could attain.

Jamie decided he wanted to be involved in wheelchair sports. He thought basketball would be the go as he had excellent hand-eye coordination and he longed to be a part of a sporting team again. Jamie's father was quick to encourage his son's dream of playing in a successful team and knew that this would be a valuable experience for Jamie's self esteem and reason for living.

Three years to the day after Jamie's football injury, his family watched proudly as Jamie wheeled himself up to the stage to collect the premiership trophy for his wheelchair basketball team. Later, Robert said to Jamie, "I always knew no matter what happened, that one day I would see you hold up a trophy for your team."

Activity 6	Reflection: Sporting Moments

❶ What are the themes in Jamie's story?

_____

_____

_____

_____

_____

_____

❷ After Jamie realised he might never walk again, he decided to concentrate on focusing on a goal other than trying to walk. Why do you think he did this?

_____

_____

_____

_____

❸ Imagine if Jamie wasn't a sporty person. What other goals might Jamie have been able to work towards to give him a purpose for living?

_____

_____

_____

_____

❹ Do you know anyone that has suffered a major injury like Jamie's? Describe their situation below.

_____

_____

_____

_____

_____

❺ How has the person tried to deal with his/her injury?

_____

_____

_____

_____

_____

_____

_____

❻ How has this person's life changed? Give details of things they can't do anymore as well as details about new things that they are involved with.

_____

_____

_____

_____

_____

❼ If an event happened that meant you couldn't do something anymore, what new things do you think you might like to become involved in? Your injury might involve the loss of the use of limbs, loss of hearing, loss of sight and so on.

_____

_____

_____

_____

_____

_____

Activity 7	A Disability In the Family

❶ Describe the disability that you or your family member has.

_____

_____

❷ What were your reactions about this change?

_____

_____

❸ How has this disability affected your family? Make sure you discuss some of the positive things that have happened as a result of the disability.

_____

_____

❹ Make a list of the things in your home and school that have had to be modified as a result of this disability. Complete the table below.

At Home

Item	Modifications

At School

Item	Modifications

The Road to Recovery

Many people who suffer a permanent injury find that their life can change emotionally as well as physically. Things that may not have seemed important before the injury, may take on a special role. Some people who have sustained injuries have become heavily involved in the development of new technologies and new ideas that would help other people with similar injuries.

Read the inspirational stories of the people below. You may have heard of some of them through their work.

Christopher Reeve

- American actor who was best known for his roles in the Superman movies (died October, 2004).

Background: In 1995, while participating in an equestrian competition, Christopher became paralysed when he suffered a spinal cord injury after being thrown from his horse.

His work: In 1999, Reeve established the **Christopher Reeve Paralysis Foundation**, which is dedicated to funding research to develop treatments and cures for paralysis caused by spinal cord injuries. This organisation also works to improve the quality of life for people living with disabilities.

Christopher Reeve raised public awareness of spinal cord injury to the world and inspired neuroscientists to develop new methods for beating diseases of the brain and central nervous system. Some of the research focuses on stem cell biology, nerve cell regeneration, rehabilitation and self-repair. He died in 2004.

Website: ▶ **www.christopherreeve.org**

Michael J. Fox

- American actor, known for roles in Spin City and Family Ties.

Background: Michael J. Fox was diagnosed with young-onset of Parkinson's disease in 1991, a secret he kept from the public until 1998 when he committed to the campaign for increased Parkinson's research.

His work: After retiring as an actor in January 2000, Fox focused his time and energy on setting up the **Michael J. Fox Foundation for Parkinson's Research**, which was launched later that year. Fox has bought Parkinson's disease to the attention of the world and he fully believes that researchers will identify what causes this disease, which will enable a cure to be developed by 2010.

Since 2000, over $35 million US dollars have been funded by the Michael J. Fox Foundation for research into finding cures for Parkinson's disease.

Website: **www.michaeljfox.org/**

Louise Sauvage

- Australian champion wheelchair athlete.

Background: Louise Sauvage was born with a severe spinal disability called myelodysplasia. She underwent 20 operations before she turned 10 and had metal rods inserted into her back at the age of 14.

Her work: Louise was determined to excel in the sporting arena and had success in swimming, basketball and athletics. As a teenager in 1988, swimming was ruled out for medical reasons and so she focused on track events.

Sporting achievements:
- *Silver medals at Athens Paralympics 2004*
- *Gold medal at Sydney Olympics 2000*
- *Gold and silver medals at Sydney Paralympics*
- *Won the Boston Marathon three times*
- *Gold medals at Barcelona(1992) and Atlanta Paralympics(1996)*

Louise has raised public awareness about athletes with disabilities. She is heavily involved in fundraising for wheelchair associations and is well known as a motivational public speaker.

Websites:
e-bility.com/articles/sauvage.shtml and **www.aspire.au.com**

Activity 8

Profile of a Survivor

☞ *Choose one of the people discussed on Page 26 and conduct some further research. You may like to use the websites provided as a starting point for your research.*

Find out as much as you can about this person and complete the profile below.

Name:

_____

Date of birth:

_____

Details of injury/disability:

_____

❶ How has this person dealt with his/her situation?

_____

_____

_____

_____

_____

_____

❷ In what ways have they raised public awareness to their disability?

_____

_____

_____

_____

_____

❸ What do you admire most about this person?

_____

_____

_____

_____

_____

❹ If you could meet this person, write down what you would like to say to them.

_____

_____

_____

_____

_____

_____

❺ Think of three questions you would like them to answer.

I. _____

_____

2. _____

_____

3. _____

_____

Jane Tomlinson: An Inspiring Story

Jane Tomlinson CBE (adapted from her website)

Jane was diagnosed with incurable, advanced metastatic breast cancer in August 2000. The disease was extensive and she was given six months to live. Over the next seven years, Jane fought through chemotherapy and drug regimes despite also developing chronic heart disease.

During this time Jane, a mother of three from Leeds, took on a series of impossible challenges, for someone suffering from cancer and undergoing chemotherapy treatment, including a full Ironman (4km Swim, 180Km bike ride and full marathon - completed inside 17 hours), two half Ironmans, the London Marathon three times, the New York Marathon, three London Triathlons and three long distance bike rides - John O Groats to Lands End, Rome to Home and her final huge challenge a 6781.8 km ride across America. Jane received numerous awards for her efforts including:

* An MBE and then a CBE from the Queen
* The Helen Rollason Award at the BBC Sports Personality of the Year Awards in 2002
* Twice recognised at the Sportswoman of the Year Awards
* A Great Briton Award
* Voted the most Inspirational Woman in Britain in 2003.
* A Pride of Briton Award in 2005

One of Jane's motives was to show that people with a terminal illness can still lead an active and fruitful life and she said "Death doesn't arrive with the prognosis." She proved to be true to her word and with her drive, unwavering determination and supreme bravery Jane provided true inspiration and genuine hope to a great many people.

Jane efforts also raised over £1,850,000 for charities including Macmillan Cancer Relief, SPARKS, Damon Runyon Cancer Research, Yorkshire Cancer Centre, Martin House Hospice, Bluebell Wood Children's Hospice and Hannah House.

Jane died in September 2007.

Group Discussion Points:

Discuss Jane's inspiring story with your classmates. Use the questions below as starting points.

❑ What goals did Jane set for herself?
❑ What goals might you set for yourself if you were in Jane; position?
❑ What factors do you think might have contributed to Jane's amazing achievements?
❑ Discuss some people that you actually know that have recovered from a serious accident or injury.

Want More? Check out these websites:

http://www.janetomlinsonappeal.com

janetomlinsonappeal.com/about/jane/index.php

Activity 9	Article: My Hero

☞ *Think of someone you know (i.e. a friend, classmate, relative) that has had to face a major obstacle in his/her life. This person may suffer from an illness or may have received a life-changing injury. Examine how his/her situation is similar to the people you have read about on Pages 26 and 28.*

Imagine you have been asked to write an article about your friend. Your story is to be published in a magazine called *Stories of Inspiration*. Think of a suitable headline for your article and start with an introductory paragraph that basically outlines what the article is going to be about. Make your article as factual as possible. You may want to talk to the person you are writing about so that you can include real details about what he/she went though as well as understanding their feelings. Be sure to include some quotes from this person. Think carefully about the sorts of questions you will ask.

Write your article in the space below and find a picture to illustrate.

• Stories of Inspiration • Special Feature •

| Activity 10 | My Story |

You have been asked to share your story with other students who are trying to cope with their disability.

Draft your story below. You may like to submit your story online using some of the websites listed on Page 13. You should be careful to either change your name or leave out your surname.

Your story should include:

- The event that caused your injury/disability
- Your feelings
- Reactions from people around you
- Happy events that have occurred in your life since your injury
- Things that helped you get through
- Books and websites that you read
- People that you talked to about your recovery
- Stories of inspiration

Teachers' Notes: Dealing with Death

Research has shown that children pass through different stages when exploring their understanding of death. Pre-primary aged children view death as something that can be reversed. This kind of thinking stems from sources such as cartoons and computer games where characters are constantly killed in a number of ways and then seemingly rise from the dead with no explanation. Children see death as temporary and impersonal and tend not to be affected by it at this time.

At junior primary level, children start to realise that death is final but they don't view it as personal. They understand that all living things die and may have experience of death through the loss of pets. Around this age, some students start to personify death by associating pictures of skeletons or angels with this idea. Some children may start to have nightmares featuring these images.

Moving towards upper primary ages, students begin to fully understand that death cannot be reversed. They understand that they too will die at some stage and some students may even become preoccupied with how they will die. Many students will start to develop their own ideas about life and death and what happens when someone dies. The big questions that many students want answers for are of course, what happens when you die? Where do you go?

As students move into teenage years, they question the meaning of life. Many will react to their fear of death using risky behaviours to display their control over their own mortality.

While each child is thought to go through stages as outlined above, it is important to remember that each child is an individual and that each child will perceive death differently, developing different perceptions, feelings and ideas. These feelings will be expressed in a unique way depending on the child and so it is difficult for a teacher to address the issues of grief and loss as a whole class. Some students may have been asking questions about death since they were a very young age while others will choose to appear unconcerned when this subject is discussed.

It is interesting to note the different reactions that students can have following an experience with death. Some students can react very strongly to the death of a pet, yet will barely acknowledge the passing of a grandparent. Other students may choose to explore death though role-play and make-believe games. Movies and novels may influence their thinking and they may start to act out death situations with their friends as part of play.

Teachers need to listen and watch students' behaviour for cues as to how to respond to a child's needs.

With younger children, it is wise to avoid phrases like "Grandma went away" and "went to sleep" as this can cause children to be fearful of anyone who says they are going away. Students may even start to become afraid of going to sleep – fearing that if they do, they won't ever wake up – just like Grandma.

When discussing death from illness, it's important to emphasise that only very serious illnesses can cause death. Students need to understand that there are many things that can go wrong with the body and these problems rarely result in death. *Source: **www.hospicenet.org***

TEACHERS NOTES •

Teachers' Notes: About Grief

Grief is a normal emotional state, which occurs after an experience of loss. Students who are grieving need to be able to communicate their feelings to a sympathetic and caring listener. The process of grief can vary among individuals but most people follow similar stages. The duration of each stage will depend on a number of factors, such as how the person died, or whether a person blames him/herself for a person's death.

The basic stages are as follows:

Emotional Stability (normal life)

Normal times leading up to the point at which a loss was experienced.

▼

Loss

Usually, a person will go into shock and possibly disbelief. They will feel numb and this stage could last a number of days.

▼

Despair

During this stage, people may feel angry or that there is no point in going on.

▼

Emotional Impact

A grieving period will follow, which can last for more than six weeks.

▼

Moving Ahead

After the emotional impact, people will start to move on. They will have intense feelings and may start to view life differently. Although there will still be constant grieving, there will be signs that the person is starting to feel better.

▼

Acceptance

Eventually, there will be a period where the person begins to accept the loss.

The road to emotional well-being:

Around this time, people will start to have normal reactions. They will continue to focus on their grief at times of anniversaries and so on, but in general they will have picked up the pieces of their lives.

About the grieving process:

It is very important that grieving students are made aware that the symptoms of grief are normal reactions and will heal with time. During periods of grief, students may experience numbness, insomnia, muscle tension, loss of appetite, depression, sadness and feelings of anger, denial, guilt and sadness.

Understand that a grieving student's academic performance and motivation may decrease during this process. This is a temporary phase and the student should return to his/her normal routine as he/she works through the process. If there are prolonged periods of moodiness, depression and changed behaviour patterns, it is best to refer the student to a school psychologist.

Samantha's Brother

Samantha Gardner was twelve years old when her mother announced to the family that she was going to have another baby. Already, there were three children in Samantha's family – her younger brother Jarrod aged nine, and little sister Carrie who had just turned three.

The Gardner children were quite excited about the prospect of a baby in the house. Carrie was too young to quite understand but Samantha and Jarrod did their best to explain to her that she wasn't going to be the baby of the house anymore. Instead, she was going to be a big sister.

Finally, the house was ready for baby number four, and Mrs Gardner was ready to have the baby any day. Samantha wondered whether it would be a boy or a girl. Since she already had a brother and a sister, she was going to be happy with anything. Jarrod desperately wished for a boy, someone to kick the footy with. He knew it would be a long way off before anything like that could happen, but he just didn't want to think about the idea of being surrounded by three girls all the time.

One morning, Mrs Gardner dropped Jarrod off at his karate lessons and then went straight into labour! Within an hour she was at the hospital and within four hours she was the proud mother of a beautiful baby boy, Ethan.

"Phew!" gasped Jarrod, after Mr Gardner told him the news. "I have a baby brother! Yee ha!"

Ethan Gardner made his way home – with Mr and Mrs Gardner, of course – to the Gardner house five days later. Samantha had been busy helping her mum clear out the study ever since her mum told her the news that there would be a new baby. She even helped paint the room and was so excited about Ethan coming home to sleep in the bassinette for the very first time. She remembered how excited she was when her mum and dad had brought Carrie home from the hospital. She could even remember the time when Jarrod was a small baby!

Every day Samantha and Jarrod would come home and rush into Ethan's nursery. Samantha had been a big help to her mum who was often still running around after Carrie. She helped her mother to bathe Ethan and would often give him his bottle at night before bedtime.

One night, not long after Ethan had been put in his cot, Mrs Gardner asked Samantha to poke her head in and see if Ethan had gone to sleep as he had been a bit unsettled earlier that evening. Samantha tip-toed to Ethan's room and quietly peeked her head through the door. Not moving from the door, she looked over at the cot and saw Ethan peacefully lying with his blue blanket neatly covering him. His eyes were closed and he seemed to be in a deep sleep.

"Well?" asked Mrs Gardner. "Has he gone down?"

"Yes, he's dead to the world," whispered Samantha to her mother, who by this stage was busy with her head in a book.

When Samantha woke up the next morning, she was surprised that she hadn't heard Ethan crying in the middle of the night. For almost five months now, he had woken her up at some stage. Most of the time he was very good but there had been the odd occasion when Mrs Gardner had been up three or four times with him. Samantha thought it was very odd that she wasn't woken up. "Must have been a very deep sleep I was in," she thought to herself.

Samantha walked out to the kitchen and saw her Aunty Anna sitting at the table. She was not looking her usual self. Aunty Anna was her mum's younger sister. She didn't have any kids of her own yet.

"Sit down Sam, I have some sad news," said Samantha's aunt.

Seconds later, Jarrod wandered out from his room and said "Mum, how come I haven't heard Ethan crying this morning?" Jarrod looked at Aunty Anna like she was an alien. "Wheres Mum?", he asked.

Their aunt explained that they hadn't heard Ethan crying because he hadn't woken up at all during the night. When Mrs Gardner woke up in the middle of the night to feed Ethan, she had gone into his room to find that he wasn't breathing. She turned on the light and saw that her little boy was not his normal colour. Aunty Anna told the children that their parents had rung an ambulance in the middle of the night and had taken Ethan to a hospital. However, it was too late for the ambulance workers to save Ethan. Ethan wouldn't be coming home.

Samantha couldn't believe what Aunty Anna had told her. She wanted to see her mum, she didn't believe Aunty Anna's story. She got up from the table and ran to Ethan's room and looked in the door. How could her beautiful baby brother be dead? He was so happy and playful yesterday afternoon.

She peered in the door and looked at Ethan's cot. It was empty. She flashed back to what she had seen last night when she checked in on him. "Dead to the world," she thought to herself. "Oh no, I should never have said that. What have I done?"

Samantha ran crying down the hallway and back out to her aunt. "Anna, it's my fault, I said he was "dead to the world", I made this happen. It's all my fault!" she wailed.

Aunty Anna reached around to hug her, "No Sam, it's OK, it's terrible news but it's not your fault darling. It is not your fault," she said to Samantha while trying to hold back her own tears.

After some examinations at the hospital, the doctors told the Gardners that Ethan's death would be written as Sudden Infant Death Syndrome on the death certificate. Samantha, Jarrod and Carrie had no idea how this could have happened. "How can you just die in your sleep? What is that all about?" demanded Samantha. She was angry with the doctors' explanation. "This makes no sense! There was nothing wrong with Ethan. Why did he die?"

The Gardner family were very sad about Ethan dying. For a long time Mrs Gardner wouldn't even leave the house. She didn't want to keep in touch with her friends who had babies either. She didn't want to go to the shopping centre and see mothers walking with their prams.

"Mummy, why don't you have another baby?" asked Carrie, "Would that stop you from being sad?"

Then one day, Mrs Gardner decided that she was going to become involved in a special organisation. She told the children that Ethan had died as a result of Sudden Infant Death Syndrome or SIDS for short.

"Does that mean you're going to wear a red nose all the time – isn't that what SIDS is about? Red Nose Day?" asked Jarrod?

"Well, that's part of it Jarrod," Mrs Gardner explained, "But I am going to help the SIDS organisation to raise money for research that will try to find out why and how these baby deaths occur. Now that I don't need to be at home all the time, I want to see how I can help these organisations and I also want to help other mothers and families who have had this happen to them. This work will help me to feel better and it will also help you and other people."

"Well Mum, if there is ANY way that I can help, tell me how because I want to feel better," said Samantha.

Aber Education

Activity 11 | Reflection: Samantha's Brother

❶ What are the themes in the story?

_____

_____

_____

❷ What was the reason for baby Ethan's death?

_____

❸ How do you think this death is going to affect the Gardner family?

_____

_____

_____

_____

_____

About SIDS

❹ What does SIDS stand for?

_____

_____

_____

❺ What did you know about SIDS before reading the story "Samantha's Brother".

_____

_____

_____

_____

❻ How can you find out more information about SIDS?

_____

_____

_____

_____

_____

_____

❼ Do you know any families that have lost a child through SIDS?

_____

_____

_____

_____

❽ Describe what happened and describe how this family has coped/changed since the event.

_____

_____

_____

_____

_____

_____

_____

What Happens When Someone Dies?

Many different things can happen depending on how a person has died. Think of a pet that you may have had. When it died, its body stopped breathing, its heart stopped beating and it's brain stopped thinking. The same happens when a human being dies. It looks as though the person may be asleep as he/she may be very still and quiet. However, this person has stopped living and will not wake up. He or she no longer needs food or water and cannot feel any pain.

Generally, when someone dies, the family members of the dead person are very busy getting everything organised for a funeral. Sometimes people can be angry, especially if the death was a horrible accident. Sometimes when the death is expected, as in the case of a long illness, there is a sense of relief. Mostly, people are very sad when they hear of someone dying, however, they may have different ways of expressing their sadness.

Remembering the person that has died

Funerals or memorial services allow family and friends to get together to remember the person that has died. At a funeral service, people talk about the person's life and they remember special things that happened in this person's life. Funerals can be held in churches, or in chapels at a cemetery. Sometimes they are held at the gravesite. A person who has died can be buried at a cemetery or they may choose to be cremated. There is usually a special place at the cemetery where you can go to remember that person once the funeral has taken place.

There are many things to be taken care of when organising a funeral and often the families of people who have died, have not had a chance to think about the death of the person as they are so busy sorting out funeral arrangements. People at funerals are often sad and many adults may be crying. This is because they are saying good-bye to the person who has died.

Family and friends often put a notice in the paper to write special memories about their loved one. This notice also lets other people know that the person has died. The family will usually place a funeral notice in the paper as well. This is an easy way for everyone to find out about the funeral and allows the person's family some time to get on with organising the service.

Feeling sad

It is normal to feel sad and it is normal to cry. You will even notice adults crying. People are sad because they know that they won't see that person again.

It can also be normal to feel frightened, especially when the person has just died. Their death may mean a very big change and you may feel that you have no one to turn to talk about this change.

Feeling angry

Sometimes when someone you love dies, you can feel very angry about this happening. You may feel that you didn't deserve this. It is OK to feel angry and you may see other people, even adults, who are angry too.

Needing answers

Most of the time, people want answers to all of their questions. You may want to know what happens to a person's body after that person dies. You may want to know if that person can still see and hear you after they have died. It is OK to ask questions but sometimes people cannot tell you all of the answers.

| Activity 12 | Needing the Answers |

When someone dies, you may feel that you want to talk to somebody about what has happened. You may want some questions answered. Sometimes those questions are difficult to answer but the best thing you can do is to talk to someone about your questions.

Make a list below of some of the questions you would like answered:

- _____
  _____
  _____

- _____
  _____
  _____

- _____
  _____
  _____

- _____
  _____
  _____

- _____
  _____
  _____

Memories Forever - A Booklet

Create a booklet (Memory book) for you to keep as a memory of the person that has died. Fill in the spaces with the person's name and add some special photos. You may even wish to draw a picture to help remember this person. Your booklet belongs to you and you do not have to share it with anyone else if you do not want to.

Instructions:

Page 1: Find a photo to stick on the cover of your Memory book. You may want to select a recent photo of this person, or you may choose to show something from another stage of his/her life.

Write down how this person fitted into your life (e.g. what was his/her relationship to you: mother, cousin, classmate, grandmother, brother etc.?).

Give details about how this person died and write down the date of their death. This date will be a special date for you in the future as it is the anniversary of that person's death. Just as we remember birthdays, we can also remember anniversaries for when people died.

Page 2: On this page, you can write down what you liked about this person. Include special memories and try to find a photo of you and the person enjoying times together. You might like to draw a picture instead.

Page 3: Write about the things that you will miss the most about this person. Draw or find a picture to illustrate.

Page 4: Find a favourite photo of this person. Explain why you have chosen this image and give details about where and when it was taken.

Page 5: Write a poem in honour of the person that has died. Try to explain some things that were unique about the person.

Page 6: Write a letter to the person. Sometimes when a person dies suddenly, we have no way of saying goodbye to them. Letters and notices in the paper can help us to express our feelings and emotions about that person's death. If the person was sick and knew that they were going to die, you may have had a chance to see them before their death. In your letter write down how you feel and take care to write some things that you may not have had a chance to say to that person when they were alive.

| Activity 13 | Memories Forever (1) |

☞ *Even though a person dies, their spirit can live on and even though that person is no longer around, you will have memories of your times together. These memories can never be taken from you.*

Create a book of memories for the person that has died. You can cut out the boxes on this page and the following pages and staple them together. Add a photo to the cover and write the name of the person. Fill in the blanks with the person's name.

1

My Times With:

_____

My relationship to them:

_____

I knew this person for _____ years.

_____ died on _____

Date of death:

_____

2

1. I liked _____ because _____

2. _____ liked me because _____

3. Some special memories of _____ include _____

_____

_____

4. Some of the things we did together were:

_____

_____

_____

Aber Education

Activity 14	Memories Forever (2)

3

What I will miss about _____

_____

_____

_____

_____

_____

_____

_____

_____

_____

4

My Favourite Photo:

This photo shows me and

_____

It is special to me because

_____

_____

_____

_____

_____

Activity 15 Memories Forever (3)

5 A Poem for _____

_____

_____

_____

_____

_____

_____

_____

_____

_____

_____

6 A Goodbye Letter to_____

Dear _____

_____

_____

_____

_____

_____

_____

_____

_____

_____

Charity Organisations (1)

Charity organisations serve a valuable function in the community. Many charities have branches across the country and even across the world. These organisations are non-profit and their work is usually committed to a cause such as cancer, poverty or domestic abuse. Many charity workers are volunteers and carry out their roles for no reward other than to see disadvantaged children lead a better life. Below is a list of charities that deal with some of the issues covered in this book.

Starlight Children's Foundation:

This organisation helps children who are seriously ill by providing entertainment programs to distract them from their pain. They are able to grant special wishes to kids and also create mobile fun centres for hospitals. These fun centres allow children to play games and watch videos from their bedside. There are about 1200 fun centres in over 540 children's hospitals around the world.

Website: ▶ **www.starlight.org**

Leukaemia Foundation:

This national organisation is committed to the care and cure of patients with leukaemia, lymphoma, myeloma, anaemia and other blood related disorders. It provides support and counselling to patients and their families, as well as providing assistance with accommodation, transportation and education. Funds raised by the Leukaemia Foundation also go towards research studies for cures and better treatments.

Website: ▶ **www.leukaemia.com**

Cerebral Palsy

Scope is the leading UK disability charity for children and adults with cerebral palsy . The main aim of this charity is to improve the lives of people living with cerebral palsy and similar disabilities. The organisation provides support and educates the community about this disease. An important role is the education of carers of people with cerebral palsy. Other roles include research into the disease and conducting national therapy workshops.

Website: ▶ **www.scope.org.uk**

Newlife

UK leading charity for disabled and terminally ill children. They provide nurse services, equipment grant services, medical research and they, like many charities, campaign. The nurse services telephone is 0800 9020095 but students are asked not to abuse this number because prank calls waste time and money. Just think how you would feel if you had an ill brother or sister and couldn't get help because some one was messing around. For more details see the website www. newlifecharity.co.uk

Dreams Come True

This is an organisation that brings joy to terminally ill and seriously ill children by helping them to fulfill their treasured dreams. There are stories on their site of people who have fulfilled their dreams by swimming with dolphins, meeting top soccer stars and pop stars

On their site, they say

'Making a dream come true for a terminally or seriously ill child will not just brighten their life, it will be a gift that their parents and family will treasure forever. That is what we do every day. We also believe that each dream, like each child is unique and precious and we operate with complete integrity and dependability - liaising, co-ordinating, organising, funding and if necessary accompanying - to ensure that the child has an unforgettable experience, and that the parents and family can share their joy.' www. dctc.org.uk

• BACKGROUND NOTES •

Charity Organisations (2)

Variety - The Children's Charity:

There is an interesting story behind the development of this international charity. In 1928, a woman abandoned her baby at the Sheridan Theatre in Pittsburgh, in the United States. The theatre owners often got together to play cards in a social club that they called "Variety", and it was during one of these games that they heard the baby crying in the empty theatre. The baby's mother had pinned a note to the baby's clothes saying that she couldn't look after the baby but had heard about the generosity and kindness of theatre people and hoped that they would look after it. The theatre owners called the baby girl Catherine Variety. They started to raise money through their social club to go towards her care. Soon after, they had raised enough money to allow them to help local orphanages by providing goods and services. Their rule was simple: they would provide goods and services but not money.

The Variety idea took off internationally and a branch was opened in Britain in 1949. There are over 80 branches of Variety worldwide. The largest event for Variety is the annual Special Children's Christmas Party, where 5000 disadvantaged and disabled children are entertained at the biggest children's Christmas party in the Southern Hemisphere.

Website: ▶ **www.variety.org.uk**

And what happened to the baby?

Well, Catherine Variety Sheridan was taken in by foster parents at the age of five. Her name was changed to Joan and she lived a happy and normal life. She served in the United States Navy during the Korean War and as a registered nurse during the Vietnam War. Joan dedicated her time to working with children and was proud of the fact that she helped start the Variety concept. She died in 1994 at the age of 66.

The Red Cross:

The Red Cross is an international organisation that helps people in a number of ways. It is involved in blood donation, raising money for special groups though the Red Shield appeal, helping the poor, and providing medical help in emergencies.

These are only some of the services that the Red Cross provides. This organisation is not run to make money, but is run to help others and that is why many of its workers are volunteers.

You can visit their websites at:

Websites: ▶ **www.redcross.org**,.uk ▶

World Vision:

World Vision helps to fight poverty by helping people change the world they live in. People are able to sponsor starving children through World Vision and much of their time is spent making sure that people in poverty have food to eat. World Vision was started in America in 1950 to help children that were orphaned in the Korean War. During the past year, World Vision helped over 50 million people in 103 countries.

Visit the World Vision sites at:

▶ **www.worldvision.org.uk**

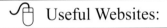 Useful Websites:

▶ **www.charitychoice.co.uk**
   - A directory of charities in the UK
▶ **www.charitiesdirectory.com,**
   www.ukcharities.org/
▶ **www.teachernet.gov.uk/wholeschool/**
   familyandcommunity/
   voluntaryorganisations/- Contains a list of charity organisations for a whole range of issues.

Activity 16 — Fun Ways to Fundraise!

☞ *Think of a charity that is close to your heart. It may be a charity dedicated to helping a cause that has affected you, a family member or a friend. Think of some of the activities you have been involved with that were designed to raise money. You may have been involved in a read-a thon, lap-a-thon or bike-a-thon, or national fundraising ideas such as Jump Rope for Heart, the 40 Hour Famine, Jeans for Genes Day, Red Nose Day and so on.*

About Your Charity:

Briefly describe what charity you will be fundraising for. Explain what this charity's main aims are and discuss why you selected this particular charity.

_____

_____

Fundraising Activities:

On the back of this sheet, list all the ideas that you can think of that would allow your class or even the whole school to raise funds for your charity organisation. Choose four of the best ideas and write notes for each heading in the boxes below.

Activity Name:_____

❶ Who will be involved?

_____

❷ What preparation is needed?

_____

❸ How will this activity be organised?
(Give brief details about the time involved, additional materials that may be required and so on.)

_____

❹ How much money do you expect to raise?

_____

Activity Name:_____

❶ Who will be involved?

_____

❷ What preparation is needed?

_____

❸ How will this activity be organised?
(Give brief details about the time involved, additional materials that may be required and so on.)

_____

❹ How much money do you expect to raise?

_____

Activity Name:_____

❶ Who will be involved?

_____

❷ What preparation is needed?

_____

❸ How will this activity be organised?
(Give brief details about the time involved, additional materials that may be required and so on.)

_____

❹ How much money do you expect to raise?

_____

Activity Name:_____

❶ Who will be involved?

_____

❷ What preparation is needed?

_____

❸ How will this activity be organised?
(Give brief details about the time involved, additional materials that may be required and so on.)

_____

❹ How much money do you expect to raise?

_____